Patterns and Formulas for Phonetic Groups in Mandarin Chinese Characters Volume 41

by

Stephen M Kraemer

In looking at Chinese characters in Mandarin, many phonetic compound/phonetic element character pairs or groups exhibit certain patterns. These phonetic patterns are based on the syllable structure of Modern Standard Mandarin, namely the syllable being composed of an initial, final, and tone. The final portion of the syllable is further composed of the rime (nuclear vowel + ending)(ending being a vowel or consonant).

(For vowel and consonant features in Mandarin, see Kratochvil 1968).

As part of the phonetic patterns given here, formulas for the arrangement of character segments (vowels and consonants) will include one or more of the six pinyin vowels and two final consonants as follows:

V1 = i

V2 = e

V3 = a

V4 = u [u]; V4 = o [u]*

V5 = ü

V6 = o [o]

C1 = n

C2 = ng

*Note: In the pinyin finals "ao," "iao," "ong," "iong," the pinyin letter "o" represents V4, the high, back rounded vowel [u]. In the pinyin finals "o," "ou," "iou{iu}," "uo," the pinyin letter "o" represents V6, the mid, back rounded vowel [o].)

In this study, four groups of phonetic characters in Mandarin will be shown. These include the 畐(fú) group, where all characters share the common phonetic element 畐(fú); the 百(bǎi, bó) group, where all characters share the common phonetic element 百(bǎi, bó); the 罢(bà, ba) group, where all characters share the common phonetic element 罢(bà, ba); and the 保(bǎo) group, where all characters share the common phonetic element 保(bǎo).

Providing information about the phonetic patterns of Chinese characters may serve to help the student of Chinese to recognize the phonetic relationship among many characters in Mandarin. Teachers of Chinese may also find this book useful in seeing how phonetic elements can be arranged to show how they share certain features of their pronunciation with other characters.

Character pronunciations are given in pinyin and are taken from Zhou You-guang (1980), based on Xin Hua Zidian (1971). Where the phonetic element character pronunciation is not found in either Zhou You-guang (1980) or Xin Hua Zidian (1971), it is taken from Handian (2004 – 2015).

畐(fú)

畐(fú)

辐(fú)

福(fú)

蝠(fú)

匐(fú)

幅(fú)

Phonetic Pattern:

Labial (f)
Totally Perfect
(fú)

(fu)
Labial V4
(V4 = u)

畐(fú)

副(fù)
富(fù)

Phonetic Pattern:

Labial (f)
Segment Perfect
(fu)

(fu)
Labial V4
(V4 = u)

畐(fú)

逼(bī)

Phonetic Pattern:

Labial (f/b)
All High Single Vowel
Finals
(u/i) [u] [i]

(fu/bi)
Labial V4 + Labial V1
(V4 = u)(V1 = i)

百(bǎi, bó)

百(bǎi)

佰(bǎi)

Phonetic Pattern:

Labial (b)
Totally Perfect
(bǎi)

(bai)
Labial V3V1
(V3 = a)(V1 = i)

百(bǎi)

䂍(bāi)

Phonetic Pattern:

Labial (b)
Segment Perfect
(bai)

(bai)
Labial V3V1
(V3 = a)(V1 = i)

百(bǎi)

弼(bì)
皕(bì)

Phonetic Pattern:

Labial (b)

Initial Perfect (b)

All Non-Mid, Front,

Unrounded Vowel Finals

(ai/i) [ai][i]

High, Front, Unrounded

Vowel (i) [i]

(bai/bi)

Labial V3V1 + Labial V1

(V3 = a)(V1 = i)

百(bǎi)

貊(mò)
陌(mò)

Phonetic Pattern:

Labial (b/m)
All Vowel Finals
(ai/o)

(bai/mo)
Labial V3V1 + Labial V6
(V3 = a)(V1 = i)(V6 = o)

百(bó)

𠶹(bāi)
佰(bǎi)

Phonetic Pattern:

Labial (b)
Initial Perfect (b)
All Vowel Finals (o/ai)

(bo/bai)
Labial V6 +Labial V3V1
(V6 = o)(V3 = a)(V1 = i)

百(bó)

彃(bì)
皕(bì)

Phonetic Pattern:

Labial (b)
Initial Perfect (b)
All Non-Low Single Vowel
Finals (o/i)

(bo/bi)
Labial V6 + Labial V1
(V6 = o)(V1 = i)

百(bó)

貊(mò)

陌(mò)

Phonetic Pattern:

Labial (b/m)
Final Perfect
(o)

(bo/mo)
Labial V6
(V6 = o)

罢(bà, ba)

罢(bà, ba)

摆(bǎi)

Phonetic Pattern:

Labial (b)
Initial Perfect (b)
All Non-Mid,
Unrounded Vowel Finals
(a/ai)
Low Vowel (a)

(ba/bai)
Labial V3 + Labial V3V1
(V3 = a)(V1 = i)

罢(bà, ba)

罴(pí)

Phonetic Pattern:

Labial (b/p)
Unaspirated/Aspirated
Stops [p]/[p^h]
All Non-Mid, Unrounded
Single Vowel Finals (a/i)

(ba/pi)
Labial V3 + Labial V1
(V3 = a)(V1 = i)

保(bǎo)

保(bǎo)

堡(bǎo)
褓(bǎo)
葆(bǎo)

Phonetic Pattern:

Labial (b)
Totally Perfect
(bǎo)

(bao)
Labial V3V4
(V3 = a)(V4 = o[u])

保(bǎo)

煲(bāo)
褒(bāo)

Phonetic Pattern:

Labial (b)
Segment Perfect
(bao)

(bao)
Labial V3V4
(V3 = a)(V4 = o[u])

保(bǎo)

堡(bǔ)

Phonetic Pattern:

Labial (b)
Initial Perfect (b)
All Non-Mid, Back Vowel
Finals (ao/u) [ɑu] [u]
High, Back Rounded
Vowel (o[u]/u[u])

(bao/bu)
Labial V3V4 + Labial V4
(V3 = a)(V4 = o[u])
(V4 = u)

保(bǎo)

堡(pù)

Phonetic Pattern:

Labial (b/p)
Unaspirated/Aspirated
Stops [p]/[p^h]
All Non-Mid, Back Vowel
Finals (ao/u) [ɑu] [u]
High, Back Rounded
Vowel (o[u]/u[u])

(bao/pu)
Labial V3V4 + Labial V4
(V3 = a)(V4 = o[u])
(V4 = u)

References

Cheng, C.C. (1973). *A synchronic phonology of Mandarin Chinese*. The Hague: Mouton.

Handian [<汉典>, '字典']. Online Chinese dictionary. (2004 – 2015). http://www.zdic.net

Kraemer, Stephen M. (1980). *Potentially pedagogically useful phonetics in the Chinese script: Their identification and characterization*. Doctoral dissertation. Rutgers University.

Kraemer, Stephen M. (1991a). *Sound clues in Mandarin character phonetic series*. Retrieved from https://scholarsbank.uoregon.edu/xmlui/handle/1794/4943

Kraemer, Stephen M. (1991b). *Levels of phonological regularity in the Chinese writing system*. Retrieved from https://scholarsbank.uoregon.edu/xmlui/handle/1794/8133

Kraemer, Stephen M. (2017). *Let's Learn Mandarin Phonics*. CreateSpace Independent Publishing Platform.

Kraemer, Stephen M. (2017). *Let's Learn Mandarin Phonics-2*. CreateSpace Independent Publishing Platform.

Kraemer, Stephen M. (2018a). *Let's Learn Mandarin Phonics-3. Rime Clue, Rime-Tone Clue, Ending Clue, Ending-Tone Clue Phonetic Patterns of Common Chinese Characters.* CreateSpace Independent Publishing Platform.

Kraemer, Stephen M. (2018b). *Let's Learn Mandarin Phonics-4. Initial Clue, Initial-Tone Clue, Tone-Clue and Related Phonetic Patterns of Common Chinese Characters.* CreateSpace Independent Publishing Platform.

Kraemer, Stephen M. (2018c). *Let's Learn Mandarin Phonics-5. Vowel Phonetic Clues for Common Chinese Characters.* CreateSpace Independent Publishing Platform.

Kraemer, Stephen M. (2018d). *Phonetic Clues for Learning Common Chinese Characters.* CreateSpace Independent Publishing Platform.

Kraemer, Stephen M. (2018e). *A Phonetic Guide to Learning Chinese Characters.* CreateSpace Independent Publishing Platform.

Kraemer, Stephen M.(2020). *Phonetic Patterns in Mandarin Chinese Characters: Pinyin "ng" Ending Finals with Unrounded Vowels*. Independent Publishing Platform.

Kraemer, Stephen M.(2020a). *Phonetic Patterns in Mandarin Chinese Characters: Pinyin "n/ng" Ending Finals with Unrounded Vowels*. Independent Publishing Platform.

Kraemer, Stephen M.(2020b). *Phonetic Patterns in Mandarin Chinese Characters: V/VC1 Finals*. Independent Publishing Platform.

Kraemer, Stephen M.(2020c). *Phonetic Patterns in Mandarin Chinese Characters: VC1 Finals with Unrounded Vowels*. Independent Publishing Platform.

Kraemer, Stephen M.(2020d). *Phonetic Patterns in Mandarin Chinese Characters: V Finals with a Rounded Medial Vowel Plus Unrounded V*. Independent Publishing Platform.

Kraemer, Stephen M.(2020e). *Phonetic Patterns in Mandarin Chinese Characters: V Finals with a Rounded Ending Vowel Plus Unrounded V*. Independent Publishing Platform.

Kraemer, Stephen M.(2020f). *Phonetic Patterns in Mandarin Chinese Characters: Labial/Velar Initials and Pinyin "m"/ "w"*. Independent Publishing Platform.

Kraemer, Stephen M.(2020g). *Phonetic Patterns in Mandarin Chinese Characters: Velar/Retroflex Initials*. Independent Publishing Platform.

Kraemer, Stephen M.(2020h). *Phonetic Patterns in Mandarin Chinese Characters: Velar/Alveolar Initials*. Independent Publishing Platform.

Kraemer, Stephen M.(2020i). *Phonetic Patterns in Mandarin Chinese Characters: Palatal Initials*. Independent Publishing Platform.

Kraemer, Stephen M.(2020j). *Phonetic Patterns in Chinese Characters: Pinyin "a/e" Variation in Mandarin*. Independent Publishing Platform.

Kraemer, Stephen M.(2020k). *Phonetic Groups in Chinese Characters: All Unrounded Vowel Finals in Mandarin*. Independent Publishing Platform.

Kraemer, Stephen M.(2020l). *Phonetic Groups in Chinese Characters: All Unrounded Vowel Finals in Mandarin Volume 2*. Independent Publishing Platform.

Kraemer, Stephen M.(2020m). *Phonetic Groups in Chinese Characters: All Unrounded Vowel Finals in Mandarin Volume 3*. Independent Publishing Platform.

Kraemer, Stephen M.(2020n). *Phonetic Groups in Chinese Characters: All Vowel Finals in Mandarin*. Independent Publishing Platform.

Kraemer, Stephen M.(2020o). *Phonetic Groups in Chinese Characters: All Vowel Finals in Mandarin Volume* 2. Independent Publishing Platform.

Kraemer, Stephen M.(2020p). *Phonetic Groups in Chinese Characters: All Vowel Finals in Mandarin Volume 3*. Independent Publishing Platform.

Kraemer, Stephen M.(2020q). *Phonetic Patterns in Mandarin Chinese Characters: Final Perfect with Palatal j/x, q/x Initials*. Independent Publishing Platform.

Kraemer, Stephen M.(2020r). *Phonetic Groups in Chinese Characters: All Unrounded Vowel Finals in Mandarin Volume 4*. Independent Publishing Platform.

Kraemer, Stephen M.(2020s). *Phonetic Groups in Chinese Characters: All Vowel Finals in Mandarin Volume 4*. Independent Publishing Platform.

Kraemer, Stephen M.(2020t). *Phonetic Patterns in Mandarin Chinese Characters: Final Perfect with Palatal j/q Initials*. Independent Publishing Platform.

Kraemer, Stephen M.(2020u). *Phonetic Patterns in Mandarin Chinese Characters: Final Perfect with Palatal Initials*. Independent Publishing Platform.

Kraemer, Stephen M.(2020v). *Phonetic Components for Meaning in Mandarin Chinese Characters*. Independent Publishing Platform.

Kraemer, Stephen M.(2020w). *Phonetic Components for Meaning in Mandarin Chinese Characters Volume* 2. Independent Publishing Platform.

Kraemer, Stephen M.(2020x). *Phonetic Components for Meaning in Mandarin Chinese Characters Volume 3*. Independent Publishing Platform.

Kraemer, Stephen M.(2020y). *Phonetic Components for Meaning in Mandarin Chinese Characters Volume 4*. Independent Publishing Platform.

Kraemer, Stephen M.(2020z). *Phonetic Components for Meaning in Mandarin Chinese Characters Volume 5*. Independent Publishing Platform.

Kraemer, Stephen M.(2020aa). *Phonetic Components for Meaning in Mandarin Chinese Characters Volume 6*. Independent Publishing Platform.

Kraemer, Stephen M.(2020ab). *Phonetic Components for Meaning in Mandarin Chinese Characters Volume 7*. Independent Publishing Platform.

Kraemer, Stephen M.(2020ac). *Semantic Compounds in Mandarin Chinese Characters*. Independent Publishing Platform.

Kraemer, Stephen M.(2020ad). *Patterns and Formulas for Phonetic Groups in Mandarin Chinese Characters*. Independent Publishing Platform.

Kraemer, Stephen M.(2020ae). *Patterns and Formulas for Phonetic Groups in Mandarin Chinese Characters Volume 2*. Independent Publishing Platform.

Kraemer, Stephen M.(2020af). *Patterns and Formulas for Phonetic Groups in Mandarin Chinese Characters Volume 3.* Independent Publishing Platform.

Kraemer, Stephen M.(2020ag). *Patterns and Formulas for Phonetic Groups in Mandarin Chinese Characters Volume 4.* Independent Publishing Platform.

Kraemer, Stephen M.(2020ah). *Patterns and Formulas for Phonetic Groups in Mandarin Chinese Characters Volume 5.* Independent Publishing Platform.

Kraemer, Stephen M.(2020ai). *Patterns and Formulas for Phonetic Groups in Mandarin Chinese Characters Volume 6.* Independent Publishing Platform.

Kraemer, Stephen M.(2020aj). *Patterns and Formulas for Phonetic Groups in Mandarin Chinese Characters Volume 7.* Independent Publishing Platform.

Kraemer, Stephen M.(2020ak). *Patterns and Formulas for Phonetic Groups in Mandarin Chinese Characters Volume 8.* Independent Publishing Platform.

Kraemer, Stephen M.(2020al). *Patterns and Formulas for Phonetic Groups in Mandarin Chinese Characters Volume 9.* Independent Publishing Platform.

Kraemer, Stephen M.(2020am). *Patterns and Formulas for Phonetic Groups in Mandarin Chinese Characters Volume 10.* Independent Publishing Platform.

Kraemer, Stephen M.(2020an). *Patterns and Formulas for Phonetic Groups in Mandarin Chinese Characters Volume 11*. Independent Publishing Platform.

Kraemer, Stephen M.(2020ao). *Patterns and Formulas for Phonetic Groups in Mandarin Chinese Characters Volume 12*. Independent Publishing Platform.

Kraemer, Stephen M.(2020ap). *Patterns and Formulas for Phonetic Groups in Mandarin Chinese Characters Volume 14.* Independent Publishing Platform.

Kraemer, Stephen M.(2020aq). *Patterns and Formulas for Phonetic Groups in Mandarin Chinese Characters Volume 15.* Independent Publishing Platform.

Kraemer, Stephen M.(2020ar). *Patterns and Formulas for Phonetic Groups in Mandarin Chinese Characters Volume 16*. Independent Publishing Platform.

Kraemer, Stephen M.(2020as). *Patterns and Formulas for Phonetic Groups in Mandarin Chinese Characters Volume 17*. Independent Publishing Platform.

Kraemer, Stephen M.(2020at). *Patterns and Formulas for Phonetic Groups in Mandarin Chinese Characters Volume 18.* Independent Publishing Platform.

Kraemer, Stephen M.(2020au). *Patterns and Formulas for Phonetic Groups in Mandarin Chinese Characters Volume 19.* Independent Publishing Platform.

Kraemer, Stephen M.(2020av). *Patterns and Formulas for Phonetic Groups in Mandarin Chinese Characters Volume 20.* Independent Publishing Platform.

Kraemer, Stephen M.(2020aw). *Patterns and Formulas for Phonetic Groups in Mandarin Chinese Characters Volume 21.* Independent Publishing Platform.

Kraemer, Stephen M.(2020ax). *Patterns and Formulas for Phonetic Groups in Mandarin Chinese Characters Volume 22.* Independent Publishing Platform.

Kraemer, Stephen M.(2020ay). *Patterns and Formulas for Phonetic Groups in Mandarin Chinese Characters Volume 23.* Independent Publishing Platform.

Kraemer, Stephen M.(2020az). *Patterns and Formulas for Phonetic Groups in Mandarin Chinese Characters Volume 24.* Independent Publishing Platform.

Kraemer, Stephen M.(2020aaa). *Patterns and Formulas for Phonetic Groups in Mandarin Chinese Characters Volume 25.* Independent Publishing Platform.

Kraemer, Stephen M.(2020aab). *Patterns and Formulas for Phonetic Groups in Mandarin Chinese Characters Volume 26.* Independent Publishing Platform.

Kraemer, Stephen M.(2020aac). *Patterns and Formulas for Phonetic Groups in Mandarin Chinese Characters Volume 27.* Independent Publishing Platform.

Kraemer, Stephen M.(2020aad). *Patterns and Formulas for Phonetic Groups in Mandarin Chinese Characters Volume 28*. Independent Publishing Platform.

Kraemer, Stephen M.(2020aae). *Patterns and Formulas for Phonetic Groups in Mandarin Chinese Characters Volume 29*. Independent Publishing Platform.

Kraemer, Stephen M.(2020aaf). *Patterns and Formulas for Phonetic Groups in Mandarin Chinese Characters Volume 30*. Independent Publishing Platform.

Kraemer, Stephen M.(2020aag). *Patterns and Formulas for Phonetic Groups in Mandarin Chinese Characters Volume 31*. Independent Publishing Platform.

Kraemer, Stephen M.(2020aah). *Patterns and Formulas for Phonetic Groups in Mandarin Chinese Characters Volume 32.* Independent Publishing Platform.

Kraemer, Stephen M.(2020aai). *Patterns and Formulas for Phonetic Groups in Mandarin Chinese Characters Volume 33.* Independent Publishing Platform.

Kraemer, Stephen M.(2020aaj). *Patterns and Formulas for Phonetic Groups in Mandarin Chinese Characters Volume 34.* Independent Publishing Platform.

Kraemer, Stephen M.(2020aak). *Patterns and Formulas for Phonetic Groups in Mandarin Chinese Characters Volume 35.* Independent Publishing Platform.

Kraemer, Stephen M.(2020aal). *Patterns and Formulas for Phonetic Groups in Mandarin Chinese Characters Volume 36.* Independent Publishing Platform.

Kraemer, Stephen M.(2020aam). *Patterns and Formulas for Phonetic Groups in Mandarin Chinese Characters Volume 37.* Independent Publishing Platform.

Kraemer, Stephen M.(2020aan). *Patterns and Formulas for Phonetic Groups in Mandarin Chinese Characters Volume 38.* Independent Publishing Platform.

Kraemer, Stephen M.(2020aao). *Patterns and Formulas for Phonetic Groups in Mandarin Chinese Characters Volume 39.* Independent Publishing Platform.

Kraemer, Stephen M.(2020aap). *Patterns and Formulas for Phonetic Groups in Mandarin Chinese Characters Volume 40.* Independent Publishing Platform.

Kratochvil, Paul. (1968). *The Chinese language today: Features of an emerging standard*. London: Hutchinson & Co., Ltd.

Xinhua zidian (New China dictionary). (1971). Beijing: Shangwu Yinshuguan. [<新华字典>, 1971, 北京：商务印书馆.]

Zhou, Youguang. (1980). *Hanzi shengpang duyin biancha* (A handy look up for the pronunciation of phonetics in Chinese characters). Jilin: Jilin Remnin Chubanshe.
[周 有光, 1980, <汉字声旁读音便查>, 吉林: 吉林人民出版社.]

www.ingramcontent.com/pod-product-compliance
Lightning Source LLC
LaVergne TN
LVHW010117170826
845678LV00012B/2460